3D SNAPSHOTS HORSES

FOG
CITY
PRESS

Published by Fog City Press,
a division of Weldon Owen Inc.
415 Jackson Street
San Francisco, CA 94111 USA
www.weldonowen.com

WELDON OWEN INC.

President, CEO Terry Newell
VP, Sales and New Business Development Amy Kaneko
VP, Publisher Roger Shaw
Executive Editor Elizabeth Dougherty
Managing Editor, Fog City Press Karen Perez
Editorial Assistant Katharine Moore
Associate Creative Director Kelly Booth
Designer Michel Gadwa
3D Illustration Andy Lackow
Production Director Chris Hemesath
Production Manager Michelle Duggan
Color Manager Teri Bell

Text Nancy Wilson Hall
Picture Research Andy Sir

A WELDON OWEN PRODUCTION
© 2010 Weldon Owen Inc.

ISBN 978-1-61628-048-2

10 9 8 7 6 5 4 3
2014 2013 2012

Printed by RR Donnelley in China

People and horses work and
play together all over the world.

We take care of horses. Horses
carry us on their strong backs
and help us with our work.

These beautiful animals have
become our very good friends.
Have you ever seen horses
like the ones in this book?

Baby horses are called foals. At first, foals like to stay close to their mothers. But soon they learn to run and play on their own.

A father horse is
called a stallion.
Stallions look
after all the horses
in the herd.

Even though they are very large,
most horses are gentle and friendly.

A horse may
have a best
friend—just
like people do.

Horses live all
over the world.
Some live in
warm places…

But they are happy in cold places,
too. In the winter their coats
grow thick to keep them warm.

A curious horse's
ears stand tall
and face forward.

Alert ears and a high tail
show that a horse is happy.

A blaze is a white stripe on the face.
White legs are called stockings.

Boy horses are called colts when they are young and stallions when they grow up.

A young girl horse
is called a filly. She
is called a mare
when she grows up.

These working
horses help
cowboys to
move cows
on ranches.

Other horses
live and work
on farms.

These horses are all saddled up.
Would you like to go for a ride?

Show horses
have their
manes and
tails brushed
and braided.

Wild horses live
on their own on
the prairie...

...or in the mountains. But
everywhere they go, horses
like to nibble on tasty grass.

Very small horses are called ponies.

A foal needs plenty of rest—just like you do.

Grown-up horses like
to relax in the pasture.

When horses play, they kick their legs high into the air.

Horses love to gallop on
their long, graceful legs.

Their manes
and tails flow
in the wind.

A strong sense of smell and
good eyesight help horses
to learn about the world.

A horse needs
lots of care.

Clean water and
lots of grass to
eat help to keep
a horse healthy.

Fences keep them
from getting lost.

So that they can be
friends with you!

Acknowledgments

Weldon Owen would like to thank the following people for their assistance in the production of this book: Diana Heom, Ashley Martinez, Danielle Parker, Lucie Parker, Phil Paulick, and Erin Zaunbrecher. 3D Conversions by Pinsharp 3D Graphics Liverpool UK.

Credits

Key t=top; b=bottom; DT=Dreamstime; iSP=iStockphoto; LO=Lucky Oliver; SST=Shutterstock

2 SST; 5 SST; 6 iSP; 8 DT; 9t iSP, b iSP; 11 SST; 12 SST; 13 iSP; 14 SST; 15t DT, b iSP; 17 SST; 18 SST; 19 SST; 20 SST; 22 SST; 23 SST; 24 DT; 25 DT; 26t DT, b iSP; 27 DT; 28 SST; 30 SST; 31t DT, b iSP; 32t DT, b iSP; 33 DT; 34 DT; 35 SST; 36 SST; 37t DT, b iSP; 38 SST; 40 DT; 41 SST; 42 iSP; 43 DT; 45 SST; 46 iSP; 47 SST; 48t iSP, b SST; 49 SST; 50 SST; 51 SST; 52 SST; 54 DT; 55 SST; 57 DT; 58t DT, b SST; 59 DT; 60 SST; 62 SST; 63 SST; 64 DT.